Who You Need to Start a Riot

Also by G.B. Ryan

Surprised by Gulls

Who You Need to Start a Riot

G.B. Ryan

ELKHOUND
NEW YORK

For Stephanie, Peter and Lincoln

For Louis

For Norma

Copyright © 2017 G.B Ryan. All rights reserved.

Acknowledgments
are due to the editors of the following journals, in which
a number of these poems first appeared.

A Lonely Riot
Degenerate Literature
Failed Haiku
Gravel
Ink in Thirds
Lowestoft Chronicle
Moonglasses
Offcourse
Picaroon Poetry
Rat's Ass Review
StepAway
The Stony Thursday Book
Tales from the Forest
Wilderness House Literary Review
Zymbol

ISBN: 978-0-692-86889-8

Printed and bound by Thomson-Shore, Inc.
7300 West Joy Road, Dexter, MI 48130
www.thomsonshore.com

Elkhound Publications
Gracie Station Box 1453
New York, NY 10028
elkhound460@gmail.com

CONTENTS

New York
Shirt Pocket, 1
Tweed, 2
Nothing to Declare, 3
Fifteenth Day of Christmas, 3
Spring, 4
Country Music Radio on Mother's Day, 5
Breaking News, 5
Recent Advances, 6
A Couple, 6
Street Sensitivity, 7
Drama, 8
Doorbell, 9
Reality, 9
Errant Son, 10
Coal, 11
Cats in the Way, 12
By Ear, 12
Sudden Recall, 13
Instructions, 13
Bacall, 14
BBC World News, 14
Poor Men Fishing, 15
Back When, 15
This Painting, 16
In the Words of Joel Oppenheimer, 16
Fantasy, 17
Free Cake, 18
Who You Need to Start a Riot, 19
Fellow Passenger, 19
Given a Lift, 20
My Opposite, 21
Kevorkian, 22
Gallery Opening, 22
A Poem Unread, 23
Maximum Security, 23
Going, 24
War Story, 24
In Memory of Caspar Henselmann, 25
What's New, 26
A Chippendale Desk, 27
At the National Enquirer, 28
Weekend Workers, 29
Metamorphosis, 29

Hawaii, 30
Health Watch, 30
First Avenue, 31
A Threat or Not, 32
Surveillance, 32
Fireball, 33
The World at Work, 34
Who Goes There?, 34
At Night, 35
Between A and B, 35
Founding Publisher, 36
No Title, 36
Screams, 37
Legacy, 38
Notice, 38
Socialists and Others, 39
Memory, 39
On Wheels, 40
Bagel Place, 40
Alert, 40
Who Is G.B.?, 41
Workout, 41
Old Man's Pride, 42
Lexington Avenue Local, 42
Provender, 43
Close Call, 43
Kayaker on East River, 44
Ladies, 44
In Years to Come, 45
Listening, 45
No Sign of Willie, 46
Photo Edit, 46
Regular Shampoo, 47

Americas
Cape Cod, 48
Winged Spirit, 48
June Mornings, 49
Country Traffic, 50
Inside Looking Out, Outside Looking In, 50
The Feast of St. Filamena, 51
Shop Talk, 52
Hate Groups, 52
Repellent, 53
Ellington in Iowa, 53
Mountain Face, 54

Little Fishes, 54
Help for Vultures, 55
Sandwich, 55
A Pack Forms, 56
Bob Hope Lives Here, 56
Freeway, 56
Target Onshore, 57
A Walk Near Guatemala, 58
The Lost Footsteps of Col. Fawcett, 59
Rio, 59
Brazilian Proverb, 59

Ireland
Lions with Lambs, 60
A White Horse at Kenmare River, 60
No Lonely Grave, 61
Koringa, the Jungle Girl, 62
Cello, 62
Near Fethard, 63
A Farmhouse Years Ago, 63
Clay Walls, 64
Neglect Bordering on Ruin, 64
Celts, 65
Two Nurses, 65
Pope George, 66
Loyal Daughter, 66
A Nice Soft Day, 67
A Monaghan Man, 67

Other Places
Midsummer Day, 68
English Hotel, 68
Unidentified Structures, 69
On First Hearing Margaret Barry, 70
Green and Orange, 71
Royal Event, 71
Whitechapel Gallery, 72
London Resting Places, 73
In the Dark, 74
Women on Bicycles, 75
City of Spectres, 75
Burgundy Afternoon, 76
A Place to Rest, 77
Old Soldier, 77

Wannabe Haiku
Wannabe Haiku, 78

Half the Fat, No Sugar
I Believe You, a Thousand Wouldn't, 82
Say Nothing and I'll Be Your Friend Forever, 83
No Dogs, No Dumping, No Loud Music, 84
Ants Attack Vatican, 85
Filling In Open Pit Mines with Plastic Cups, 86
Press 1 for English, 87
Is You or Is You Ain't?, 88
Become a New You, 89
Think You're in Heaven but You're Living in Hell, 90
You Have Been Preselected, 91
From the Comfort of Home, 92
No Bad Language, Erotica, Violence, Nothing Disturbing, 93
Amish Country Cage-Free Large Brown Eggs, 94

New York

SHIRT POCKET

There is beach sand in the breast pocket of his white shirt.
He can't remember when he wore it last. What was he
doing on a sand-covered beach in a fish-white shirt?

Was it the time he walked with that beautiful woman
down by the water after dinner beneath the palms?
How long ago was that? He didn't own this shirt then.

It is definitely beach sand. Unless some person
has troubled to produce a convincing replica.
It is possible he is losing his memory.

He intends to look in his pockets from time to time
for items that indicate he indeed has been in
places that do not immediately come to mind.

TWEED

In days when men who worked in publishing houses
wore tweed suits, I wore a heathery tweed that would
not die. I threw away the pants when the legs frayed.
Years later I wore the tweed jacket and blue jeans
into I forget the name on Sixth Avenue.

A man with eyeglasses pushed high on his forehead
and a tape measure draped around his shirt collar
gazed at the jacket, tested a lapel and said,
This you purchased from us.

He said he remembered buying the bolt of cloth
on a rocky isle off the west coast of Scotland
after crossing rough seas in a tiny ferry.

Stonechats, wheatears, red-beaked choughs playing in the air
and calling to one another, gannets diving
and great gray seals watching with their brown doglike eyes.
(Details supplied by me.}

After talk with a weaver in a stone cottage
and more negotiations over smoky malts
in the harbor pub, all parties reached agreement
the bolt of cloth would make its way to the New World.

On his trip back to the mainland, the waves were high
and he nearly broke his arm against a bulkhead.
The heathery tweed showed up at Sixth Avenue.

He hadn't thought about this cloth in a long time.
Now, if I didn't mind, he needed to sit down.

NOTHING TO DECLARE

Green for Nothing to Declare:
a customs agent beckoned
and had me open my bag.

He found nothing and nodded.

In my twenties, I told him,
I frequently used to be
examined but this had not
happened me in quite a while,
what made him stop me today?

Federal regulations
did not permit him to tell,
but he could guess, sad to say,
whatever made them stop me
in my twenties was not what
made him delay me today.

FIFTEENTH DAY OF CHRISTMAS

Outside a tall building
in mid January
a tree stands in flower.

Its roots soaked in hormones?
A steam pipe underneath?
Is it global warming?

The wintry sun catches
plastic unlit blossoms
of wired decorations.

SPRING

1
In frigid cloud-enshrouded March
in apprehensive tone of voice
a radio announcer claimed
only minutes ago he'd seen
on his way to the studio
a big yellow thing in the sky

2
It's getting near mid April
and I think I must agree

that with no blooms or leaves
and hardly any buds

the trees, with idle branches,
look as if they have connived

to take a year off work

3
Enjoying a warm April afternoon
a skin and bone body on a park bench
strokes his or her miniature dog's head
protruding from adjoining nylon bag

4
His bicycle leaned against the wire mesh fence,
which he had somehow managed to climb over.

About eighty, white hair neatly cut, a tie,
he sat at the base of a flowering tree,

pink cherry, with many daffodils around.

The song he sang might have been a madrigal
or something formal in another language,

although you would have to say his voice was weak.

COUNTRY MUSIC RADIO ON MOTHER'S DAY

Listening to country music radio
on Mother's Day is a radical thing to
do. One mother would never close her eyes till
all of her teenage kids came home, regardless
of the hour. Years on, when it was time to go
she lingered on and she said she could not leave
until all of her kids came home one last time.

The last one there, to make a guess, was the guy
doing the song, who sounds like he might have been
on a tour of Alabama roadhouses.

So, now that her sons and daughters had gathered
around her bed in her home, what did she do?
She died with our Savior's name upon her lips.

BREAKING NEWS

Enormous numbers of golden brown butterflies
fly north out of Mexico over the border.
For what purpose? Why are they coming? To breed. True!
Swarms arrive in our country with one thing in mind –
to have sex and lay eggs and leave caterpillars.

RECENT ADVANCES

I hear researchers can now assign
particular neurotransmitters
to specific lines of poetry
and ID the hormones borne in blood
responsible for verbal constructs.

Think what this does for diagnosis.

Seeing a poem, an editor
will now have time to warn the poet
of a medical emergency.

A COUPLE

From up here I see their backs and both may be
gone twenty but little more. He flops around
almost like a child while she takes little steps
and is in control of their trajectory.

In years to come she will call attention to
speed limit signs or approaching traffic lights
and he will wave a hand or just shake his head
about to say please leave the driving to me.

STREET SENSITIVITY

1
When two of them collided
each ignored the other and
went his way without a word:
it was nothing personal.

I would have put my money
upon an instant showdown:
curses, insults, quick punches,
kicks while down, nothing fatal.

These guys avoided conflict:
there would always be a time
good to pick a fight worth while —
and not a loony attack.

2
Did I see aggression
where none was intended?

A lack of good manners
unnoticed by one with
a lack of good manners
I saw as aggression.

He lay on the sidewalk,
his look was bewildered,
he had no idea
what made me put him there.

It had been a random
attack, someone deranged.

DRAMA

A thin agile man in his late twenties
confronted four men in their late thirties,
all beefy guys used to physical work,
one of them superintendent of a house
across the street.

They may have objected to his chaining
his bike to the rail outside the building.

The superintendent advanced upon him
and the thin agile man jumped in the air
and with the toe of his right shoe firmly
tapped the big superintendent in the chest
and landed in good balance on his feet
as the heavyset man hit the asphalt
on his back like a feather dropped by wind.

The big man sat up and watched the thin man
unlock his bicycle and ride away.

The other three could easily have rushed
him and presumably overcome him.

They did not move.

I think we all felt a small tap in the
solar plexus.

DOORBELL

My doorbell is pressed downstairs
at an early morning hour,
someone who can't find his keys
pushing his hand on most of the bells,

someone who sees himself as
a lovable fun person
who shares an environment
with unlovable nonfun persons.

I remember when I was
a lovable fun person
who had friends to remind him
of how often he could be
an unlovable nonfun person.

REALITY

On a bench high above
the East River, folded
jacket and pants, white shirt,
watch and wallet on top,
black shoes placed to one side.

No sign of any note.

I look down at water,
coiling and fast moving.

A man behind a tree
adjusts his camera.

His smirk appears to ask:
what would you have done if
you had not noticed me?

ERRANT SON

The Lexington Avenue local
opened its sliding doors as I passed
the turnstile and rushed to catch the train.

While his mother used her turnstile card,
a boy about three years old escaped
underneath and ran toward the train.

He stood inside the automatic
open doors and smiled expectantly
back at his screaming, running mother.

She and I crossed the platform and got
inside just before the doors slid shut
and the train roared forward on its tracks.

About four stops later, I noticed
that she was still clinging to the child
on her lap and weeping soundlessly

while he tried to extricate himself
from imprisoning arms, impatient
yet pleased in his mother's loving grip.

COAL

1
In Liverpool just after the Beatles
the nineteenth century imitation
Greek and Roman temples that would endure
beyond the Empire were startlingly black.
A fingertip made lines on a white shirt.
There was soot in the air. The sheep were black.

2
In greater Atlanta suppose
every gasoline and diesel
vehicle becomes electric
tomorrow and raises levels
of carbon dioxide in air
because of the increased demand
on power stations fired by coal.

3
Are we on a path to become a multiplanet species
or not? asks Elon Musk If we're not … we'll simply be hanging out
on Earth until some eventual calamity claims us.

The first humans to emigrate to Mars
are our best hope for the survival
of our species, says Stephen L. Petranek.

Sooner or later we must expand beyond this
blue and green ball, or go extinct, says Chris Impey.

If it's too expensive to process effluent coal smoke
will an exodus to Mars be a cheaper way to go?

CATS IN THE WAY

Cats lie in doorways oblivious.
They don't believe they are camouflaged,
they don't play dead and they are rarely
belligerent things unaccustomed
to give way. Dogs, rabbits and mice see
and understand. But not cats. They all
stay where they are, even the smart ones.

Cats have been watching since Egyptians
built the pyramids. The problem is
what we do makes little sense to them.
If you point at something for a cat
it looks at the tip of your finger.

BY EAR

A knowledgeable person might have named
the Italianate rustic style in which
the house was built and might have known why it
was close to railway tracks. The local stop
was gone – this had been the station house – but
not the trains, they sped by and shook the house.
She said her husband and she no longer
noticed them, although once he had woken
and asked what had happened to the five-ten,
it had not passed through. That day no trains came.

We come in low over suburban roofs
at an early morning hour, do they wake?
Too many flights for them to miss one plane.
Do they ever wander their silent homes
saying yes they've heard the airport is closed?

SUDDEN RECALL

No matter how long
and descriptive or
on the other hand
coded and oblique

what diary can
match an unwritten
found unexpected
motel ballpoint pen?

INSTRUCTIONS

Please take this shamrock to President Obama.
It will surprise him since it's not St. Patrick's Day
or he may assume it must be once he sets eye
on shamrock if he recognizes it as such.
If you decide to fly to Washington DC
you can fool sniffer dogs by putting the shamrock
in a ziplock plastic bag. Please try not to be
ostentatious, but you and I differ on this.
At the White House, don't jump the fence and sneak inside.
They might shoot you. Join a group and leave the shamrock
somewhere Barack will find it. I'll write him later.

BACALL

Lauren Bacall, long after her book
appeared, from time to time, unannounced
came by her publisher's ladies' room.

An editorial employee
very young but beautiful and tough
much in the way of Lauren Bacall
told me she lingered there to observe
what the great star would put on her face.

Bacall snarled, Get the hell out of here.

How had Bacall-to-be responded?

She said, I got the hell out of there.

BBC WORLD NEWS

The BBC reporter in Athens
covering the Greek financial crisis
when first we saw him was white and timid
and behaved as if he felt out of place.

As the weeks passed with Greek politicians
in irate endless negotiations
the BBC reporter in Athens
unbuttoned his shirt and worked on his tan.

The blue sky, the sun, his deepening tan
and the Parthenon over one shoulder
made it hard for TV viewers to grasp
the worsening hardship of Greek people.

POOR MEN FISHING

Poor men on a river bank or ocean pier
catch and keep tiny fish to consume alone
in a smelly room, and some have memories.

When in the mood to talk one might say to you,
You never know what a place is truly like
until you have to make some money in it.

You say you understand but circumstances –
he is not listening, he has fish to catch.

BACK WHEN

The sound was off and there were no subtitles,
people were talking and no one was watching
except me the live color interiors
of ruins that cut away to black-and-whites
of groups of people eating and drinking who
looked as if they might be preparing for war
or perhaps honoring a local saint but
recognizably under ceilings of what
became picturesque ruined interiors.

These were not Tudors or Elizabethans
in the stark black-and-white flashback stills, they were
people whose hairstyles and clothing were not all
that different from ours, and it hit me to see
colorful wildflowers and moss on the stones.

THIS PAINTING

I do not like this painting. Move on,
you say, and look at something else.
Since it is hung here in this museum
the painting may be better than you think.
If it's OK, it's you who are at fault.

Before I move and look elsewhere
I concede this painter I do not like
has imagination. Everyday
imagination surprises us
with an insight or description.

He has that and also talent
in handling brush and colored paints
plus a knowledge of what has gone before.

Imagination ... talent ... knowledge ...
I do not like this painting. Move on,
you say, and look at something else.

IN THE WORDS OF JOEL OPPENHEIMER

People think I am someone
who can be friendly one day
and can ignore you the next,
the kind that runs hot and cold.

Look how thick these lenses are.

Thing is, I don't see your face –
but say Hi Joel to me,
I will know you by your voice.

FANTASY

You don't own me.

                        I never thought I did.

You've certainly behaved as if you did.

That was only fantasy.

                        You believe
in fantasy?

          Only to do with you.

It's in your mind, nothing to do with me.

I fantasize that you want only me.

Because I am attractive to others
and they come after me.

                        Indeed they do.

You know what people say about water –
drink your fill but don't drown.

                        I think I drowned.

You think?

          Where will I find a woman as
beautiful as you?

            That's all in your mind –
treat any woman as beautiful and
she will fulfill your wildest fantasy.

And if I do not think her beautiful?

That is caused by your lack of fantasy.

FREE CAKE

I visited her apartment
after work in a suit and tie,
and the doorman once he knew me
merely gestured to the elevator.
But one day he did not let me enter
when I wore faded jeans and a T-shirt.
I said that I had seen people
enter wearing similar clothes.
He knew my voice. By sight, he had
not recognized me. He apologized.

A block north of Lincoln Center
(the Metropolitan Opera House}
there used to be a record store
on Broadway. Outside it one afternoon
a bearded man in a Hawaiian shirt
cut a slice from a huge sponge cake,
ceremoniously placed it
on a paper plate with a plastic fork
and offered it to passersby,
saying that this was his birthday.

Although he stood at a table
on the sidewalk a block north of
the Metropolitan Opera House,
people would not have expected
to see Luciano Pavarotti
clad in a blue Hawaiian shirt
putting a slice of yellow cake
on a paper plate with a plastic fork,
even if they knew it was his birthday.
Not one of them recognized him.

WHO YOU NEED TO START A RIOT
(*after Mark Granovetter*)

One, someone who will throw a rock
if provoked before a window.

Two, someone who will throw a rock
if somebody else throws one first.

Three, someone who will throw a rock
if the others throw their rocks first.

Four, someone who will loot the store
if the others break the window.

FELLOW PASSENGER

A man in a suit, about thirty,
sitting next to me in a slow bus,
loudly and incessantly expounds
on takeovers, buyouts, rate changes
and so forth, sufficient to make me
wonder whether there is anyone
on the other end of the phone call.
There seems to be someone. But why is
this loudmouth in an expensive suit
sitting in a slow truculent bus
next to someone like me? He expounds
on hedges, economic slowdowns,
index funds, low risk blue ribbons. Fuck!
He quickly glances, then continues.
Loudly and clearly I repeat: Fuck!
I have to go, the man tells his phone,
you may have heard, I have a problem.
He gives me a sidelong look and asks,
Are you satisfied now? I say, Yes!

GIVEN A LIFT

As he drove the car
it was annoying
and then alarming
how she said to him
at the traffic lights:
It's red. It's turned green.

In a while she said,
It takes both of us
together to drive.

As he drove the car
were things black and white
like an old movie?

Or yellow and blue
like under water?

MY OPPOSITE

On a floor of a neighboring highrise,
a dog (a terrier, I think) has been
yapping nonstop from eight in the morning,
when its owners abandon it for work,
till six in the evening, when they return.

If it came from an animal shelter,
until now it has never been alone.

Ten hours' nonstop barking, three days of this,
I would have said it is not possible.

A filibustering politician
can allow himself a glass of water.
Not this dog. No granules of food either.

And then on the fourth day there is silence.

Have they had its vocal chords cut or has
it ended in the river? It may have
been returned to a local Puppy Land.

I tell a friend about this and she says,
You should know that dog is your opposite:
when you're left alone you quieten down,
you do your barking with people around.

KEVORKIAN

She would have been more comfortable
with Ralph Lauren or with Calvin Klein
than with Dr. Jack Kevorkian.

How was she going to get through lunch
with a man who said he enabled
sick people to terminate their lives?

She took him to a French restaurant, which
he refused to enter, pointing to
a yellow M down the avenue.

This place is amazing, she enthused,
I've never been in a McDonald's
before, I just can't believe I'm here!

Was it an act or was she sincere?
After all she was a journalist.
He was where he demanded to be.

GALLERY OPENING

I do not remember the name of the gallery
below ground level on I think it was Mercer Street.

After visitors came down a flight of metal steps
they saw wine on their left and plates of food on their right.

Glass in hand, you could watch them descend the metal steps
and forecast which way individuals would first turn.

When you were sober you could get a very high score.

A POEM UNREAD

What's your expectation
of a poem unread?

Love? A striking painting
can catch you by surprise.

Not a poem unread.

You have to work to read,
decide to read the thing
with what expectation?

Love? You see the fountain
in your garden or brick
wall outside your window.

What you do not see yet
is a poem unread.

MAXIMUM SECURITY

Four walls, a floor, a ceiling, neon light,
twenty-three hours solitary, one hour
a day outside the cell for exercise.

What would we do with no one to talk to?
Can this be why at times we wake in fright
at all the steel and concrete in our day?

GOING

Ask what keeps us going.
We drive up close, slow down,
it's death keeps us living.

Death a motel that keeps
a light in the window,
where we shower and sleep.

When you are near you smell
her skin and then you feel
her magnetic fingers.

WAR STORY

Gettysburg sounds like it might have been
in World War II, you could look it up.

When the woman said that as a child
in London she had been terrified
by German bombs, people looked at her
as if somehow she had just stepped out
of a Matthew Brady photograph.

In an undertone a man told those
standing near him at the opening
that she had been a child commando.

She had landed by glider behind
German lines in Normandy, a blade
held crosswise in her tiny white teeth.

SS men patted her head and died
like pigs, squealing in their own warm blood.

It was minutes before the story
got back to her. Even then there were
those who nodded at her denials.
What could she be expected to say?

IN MEMORY OF CASPAR HENSELMANN

Caspar and Van,
Xavier and Sam,
the Henselmanns.

West Coast beware,
the Henselmanns
have all moved there.

Van and Cas forever New York:
friends, dinners and country visits
and often the unexpected
as well as some nice surprises
flow in a stream of consciousness.
Van and Cas: different people
who could make different people
feel at home. Food was delicious.

As you know, Xavier and Sam both
at present are busy founding
with Andrea and Jessica
a generation in the sun.
All got to spend time with Caspar.

I think of visits to New York
of Caspar's sister Beatrice
and of Caspar's father Albert.

Caspar had a dangerous side.

Few who contemplated his art
realized his abstract concepts
on pedestal or wall all came
from jagged steel, molten plastic,
inconceivable gas and flame,
highly dangerous to be near.

As a driver, he was ready
for Sebring and Talladega,
as well as being pinned between
old houses in a narrow lane
in a deserted French village.

Afternoon in Connecticut,
before we eat the wild mushrooms
we have gathered in the woods, should
I say goodbye to my children?

Every one of us here today
can recall a positive thing
that Caspar did for us unasked.
Some of us who knew him for years
could make a list, because he was
a giving person who reached out
to us when he could. He was one
of a kind who enjoyed himself
helping others enjoy themselves.

Caspar has now passed through our lives.
We are fortunate to have known
a man so generous to us.

WHAT'S NEW

Her belt is hanging
from a single loop
and I tell her this.

She gives me a look.

I ask, Is the belt
meant to hang that way?

She gives me a look.

Mental note: watch for
young women with belts
hanging from one loop.

Know what the trends are.

A CHIPPENDALE DESK

A Chinese desk,
obviously
it's Chippendale,
a nice piece but
nothing special
yet worth a lot.

And look at this,
my favorite
in all the store,
you think it's weird,
I think so too
but Chippendale.

It's great, it's rare,
but marketwise
it's worth much less
than a piece that's
obviously
a Chippendale.

People who buy
a Chippendale
want it to look
all Chippendale,
like those who buy
a Cadillac.

AT THE NATIONAL ENQUIRER

This is Mr. Sinatra,
let me speak to Mr. Pope.

Ah, Mr. Sinatra, you
want to speak to Mr. Pope.

Mr. Pope shaking his head.

Sorry, Mr. Sinatra,
he is not in the office.

He walked into that office
less than five minutes ago.

You know that he walked in here
less than five minutes ago.

Generoso Pope puts out
his hand for the telephone.

I offer him privacy
but Mr. Pope shakes his head.

Hi Frank, sure Frank, see you soon,
he hangs up and then he says:

Kill the Sinatra story.

WEEKEND WORKERS

The parrot called to her until she
answered, and then reassured the bird
continued to hunt from desk to desk
running along tops of dividers
in the empty open-plan office
for things to eat or things to play with.

The white cockatoo allowed his crest
to fall open petal by petal
and screamed at me with a sideways look
but we knew each other and wasted
no time from our personal pursuits.

Her big apartment was L-shaped and
when she was home and he was awake
but could not see her he kept in touch
through his frequent calls, which she answered.

And outside on Broadway I will walk
voiceless and probably heedless of
the brightly plumaged chattering flocks.

METAMORPHOSIS

It came as a shock when the young woman
with straight yellow hair below the shoulder
sitting demure in the bus suddenly
wrestled with demons in the air above
who twisted her hair in a ropelike hank
and let it hang down in a ponytail

HAWAII

Say Hawaii and I recall
the woman in a bikini
who assumed a suggestive pose
beside a sleeping green turtle
and think macadamia nuts
in dark chocolate or sea salt

HEALTH WATCH

A diminishing testosterone
level in the blood can drive a man
crazy who has been sane up to this.
Men should therefore watch for warning signs.

Could the hawks and falcons that I spot
be only violent fantasies
to compensate for sinking levels?

Peregrine, redtail, even merlin
numbers are up I hear with relief
although it's hard on pigeons and rats.

FIRST AVENUE

As I stroll northward up First Avenue
three or four pigeons
walk next to me in the same direction.
It appears as if
I am taking the air with my pet birds.

The gulls above are
circling on an invisible spiral,
taking easy glides
to enjoy the urban experience.

A guy on a bike
plays just beyond the reach of snapping cars.
His life depends on
drivers with good peripheral vision
and quick reflexes.
Perhaps he is one of the immortals
or believes he is.

Three black sports utility vehicles
flashing colored lights
escort another of their kind unlit
with clouded windows.
A United Nations diplomat hides
inside bulletproof.
I hear the number of cars indicates
the person's status.

As I stroll northward up First Avenue
pigeon companions
walk next to me in the same direction.

A THREAT OR NOT

A married pair of psychiatrists (don't joke)
noticed how any two people in one place
can react differently to an incident:

to one it is a threat and heart beats faster,
to the other it is insignificant.

You could say the stress is in the perception.

SURVEILLANCE

1
People at videos monitor you as you enter
an airport terminal, as they do in big casinos.
They do not wait for you to join the security line,
as they do not wait for you to join a gaming table.
From the start they watch your every move, who you talk to, who
you brush against, what you drink, what you read, all of your moves,
before you think they have even thought about watching you.

2
How can they monitor people in the summer rush
at JFK? They might as well watch bees in a hive.
During busy times they depend on information.
A retired agent in a hospital bed told me
the men at the passport desks are the ones who receive
electronic data on incoming passengers
and push a button on you before you clear your bags.
Traffickers buying freedom or looking for revenge
give data, and so do furriers and jewelers
in Europe who seek the ten percent bounty on goods
seized by customs when not declared for import duties
by women who remove the labels or wear the stones.

3
When three men on a London street demanded money
from me I backed away from them fast and they followed
until they stopped as if they hit glass across the street.
I was amazed but did not linger. I went back and
saw the CCTV camera above and guessed
that they dared not trespass into its magic aura.

FIREBALL

Looking north from a window over the East River,
I saw a big fireball, its tail almost vertical,
at ten to one on Tuesday morning. It disappeared
behind the highrise buildings near the river around
72nd Street, a white teardrop. I listened
for the crash, heard nothing, waited for the police and
ambulance sirens, heard nothing – another early
morning incident that passed unnoticed but somewhere
a metallic or stony lump lay too hot to touch
that someone would throw in a bin in the afternoon.

But I had seen it and the cat had witnessed it too.
One day I would say to her, Remember that fireball?
And she would say, Wow.

Huge Fireball over Northeastern US, Google said
later that day, and we recognized our private bit
of planetary theater had been invaded.
It fell in Maine and not on 72nd Street.
I was not drunk. The cat was not imagining things.

THE WORLD AT WORK

I used to see him sitting at a desk
in a window across an open space
looking at a computer monitor
and busily tapping on a keyboard,
which he did for eight or nine hours a day.

The most I managed was four or five hours
and I would not have achieved even this
had I not the goad of his industry.

It never occurred to me that he might
only have been playing video games.

On a bus the other day I noticed
I was the only one not looking at
a telephone and fingering a pad.

Who can they be texting, and what about?

As for myself, I have nothing to say
and just about no one to text it to.

WHO GOES THERE?

Caspar Henselmann
gave me a sculpture,
a length of painted
zigzag sheet metal
too long for a cab.

People said hello
to me on the street,
as if it were a
recognizable
cultural symbol.

It's a matter of
personality
which you prefer – to
hold a lightning bolt
or carry a cross.

AT NIGHT

As the bell in the great clock bangs midnight
Yeats alone in a tower awaits a ghost
with two long glasses brimmed with bubbling wine,
one for him to drink, one for a ghost to breathe.

A hundred years later poet Carrie Shipers writes
of telling her son there is no monster under his bed
and if the monster is lonely after the child sleeps
he can find her alone downstairs at the kitchen table.

BETWEEN A AND B

Metal tables with umbrellas,
corrida posters in black frames,
a plywood bar, a ground floor room
in a courtyard on East Third Street,
even then these were out of style
but since I had no furniture
it could work as my apartment.

People hit the door and shouted
from two to six every morning
and often would not leave because
I could not lock them out if they
came all this way to buy a drink
but once they had a look inside
they were always willing to go.

FOUNDING PUBLISHER

An elderly man with a bushy mustache,
striped blazer and clean boater who could have watched
cricket in Kent stood in an elevator
of a highrise building on East 50th.

An editor announced in a soothing tone:
This elevator stops first on the twelfth floor.
He stood in front of the buttons and no one
bothered to argue at nine in the morning.

The old gent got off at Knopf on the twelfth floor.
The editor explained: That was Alfred A.
He still visits and he doesn't tolerate
the elevator stopping on early floors.

NO TITLE

Irish for deceit
uisce fe thalaimh
water underground

gaire Sean doite
scalded John's laughter
denying he hurts

even better is
the word in Finnish
pilkunnussija

for comma fucker
someone too aware
of punctuation

SCREAMS

We were outside a school
when she became alarmed
by loud screams that sounded
like a panicking horde.

Kindergarten playtime,
I said. They've been quiet
for hours and need release.

Still unconvinced, she said,
Hard to imagine these
terrible screams coming
from small happy children.

I told her that one time
near an English village
I woke at dawn to screams,
many and agonized.
I had not seen when I
arrived the night before
the sign for Parrot World.

She said, I'd have freaked if
I heard things scream at dawn.

I agreed, screams can be
much easier to take
later on in the day.

LEGACY

I sat next to two elderly women on a bus. One had
a cat in a fabric carrying case,
which was jumping around, agitated.
I said cats do not make good travelers.
Mine doesn't mind, she said, pushing down on its squirming body.
This caused two of us to exchange a glance.

After the cat owner got off, the remaining woman said
she had a cockatoo. She held her hand
up to show it had bitten her fingers.

I said cockatoos can live to eighty.
Mine is thirty, she went on, and I worry what will happen
after I am gone. My son would take it
but his wife – she's a lawyer – she says no.
There's a nice Filipino family on another floor
and the bird comes from somewhere over there.
I copied their name from their mailbox and
gave it to my daughter-in-law to make a change in my will.
The gift will be a big surprise for them.

NOTICE

It can be reassuring to read
next to a red fire extinguisher
the name of the one responsible
on that floor of the office building
for evacuation of the staff
in the event of an office fire.

I remember surprise on reading
my name next to fire extinguishers
at a publishing house where I worked.

After I mentioned this at a lunch
a current employee phoned to say
my name was still on the notices
although I had not worked there for years.

Now we know where to find you, she said,
in the event of an office fire.

SOCIALISTS AND OTHERS

From time to time during a hard winter
I helped women distribute sandwiches
on the Bowery for Dorothy Day
from a Catholic Worker Movement van
because these were gifts with no questions asked
for working men who were down on their luck.

I looked on myself as a socialist,
not a Catholic, though I could admit
Christians went where socialists feared to go.

A man whose loft was on the Bowery,
Mark Rothko, used to complain about how
the country was run. I once suggested,
Why not give away cash as you see fit
to those in need, since you now have money?

You're not a real socialist, he said,
you're what I might call a philanthropist
(only he said fucking philanthropist),
you're talking about personal power
over people instead of a nation
organized on socialist principles.

Dorothy Day had her opinions too,
often about people who volunteered.
I claimed that a woman I was assigned
to accompany had no need of me –
she had loyal protectors on the street
who would attack or kill anyone she
pointed at, including me. Be careful,
Dorothy answered with less than a smile.

MEMORY

I went to visit her in hospital
and brought along a six pack of pale ale,
a gift that simply made her roll her eyes.

Another guy held in one hand a shoot
of open bird of paradise flower.
She never forgot, and neither have I.

ON WHEELS

Girls you might think hardly old enough to walk
in small helmets and colorful scooter clothes

speed at the level of your rheumatoid knee
followed by trotting anxious calling mothers.

These new women who ride the city sidewalks
will make a novel challenge to their new men.

BAGEL PLACE

The old bagel place with the plastic chandeliers,
a window full of tall unflowering plants and
workers who looked like they had served seven to ten

has been replaced by a stark illumination,
an aquarium box with people who say Hi,
but the bagel and scallion cheese remains the same

ALERT

Men in black dangle on ropes
from army helicopters
high above water level

muscular activity
at which we know we excel

but don't know how to prevent
a fifteen year old in Tomsk
from hacking the Pentagon

WHO IS G.B.?

Who is G.B. Ryan?
My first name is George, there
are too many Georges
who put pen to paper.

There's a star typographer,
a chess master in Dublin,
a Vatican defender
among several others.

There's a George Ryan Square
in the South Bronx and to
have something named for you
in that part of this town

you have to be a bad ass
or even qualify for
crimes against humanity
to be honored by a square.

My answer to you is
be careful what you say.
They may not have nailed him.
He could still be around.

WORKOUT

She was riding a bicycle fast
and holding at the end of a leash
some kind of miniature puffball
bred to occupy half a cushion.

I felt sorry for the tiny brute,
little legs whirring like machine parts,
till I saw the handlebar basket
lined with soft white towels to conduct
the reigning miteweight champion home.

OLD MAN'S PRIDE

It's hard on a guy in
a bus offered a seat
by a younger woman.
Thanks, I prefer to stand.

Pass me on a staircase
and I'll admire your butt.
Don't ask to take my bag.

But if you see me fall
don't leave me there to die.

LEXINGTON AVENUE LOCAL

When hindered from automatically closing
the subway doors sound an electronic ding dong.

Someone holding a door open may be causing
this series of ding dongs and reopening doors.

But I have heard, I tell a woman sitting next
to me, that some train drivers grow excessively
fond of and prolong the sounds deliberately
and are suspended on full pay during rest and
treatment for this emotional aberration.

But she is young and skeptical and merely shrugs.

PROVENDER

A nineteenth century American
kept an iron pot of stew simmering
over a low fire and served visitors
from a ladle to a bowl. Uncooked meat
and vegetables brought by the guests were
dropped in the stew for future consumption.

A version of simmering pot lives on
today in a friend's refrigerator,
from which I was told to help myself to
any or all the cooked items preserved
in plastic bags or wrapped in foil, with none
identified and none with any date.

Another friend warned against eating things
from the freezer, saying she was certain
she had seen things there two years earlier.

CLOSE CALL

She steps in front of a bus,
which jerks to a halt a foot

from her face and telephone.
She steps back on the sidewalk

with no interruption of
whatever she is saying.

Might be at peace with the Lord,
ready to meet her maker.

Or, as Hemingway would say,
could be grace under pressure.

And then, putting thought aside,
there's just plain orneriness.

KAYAKER ON EAST RIVER

Someone is paddling a kayak down the middle
of the East River, much too far out to assign
a gender but I guess male from the reckless course
taken down the middle of this barge-infested
waterway of weaving tidal countercurrents.

I was on a sailboat with an outboard motor
once in a harbor mouth facing down an ocean
going freighter, fast approaching and blasting air
from a horn at us, since it could not stop or veer
to one side to avoid us. At the last moment
our helmsman steered aside, gunned the outboard motor,
pleased with having shaken his fist at the mighty.

I assume the kayaker on the East River
is an idiot of some kind. The watermen
will claim they never saw him, and it is even
possible on open water they talk the truth.

LADIES

You expect old men to be tough and glittery-eyed
but there are so few of them and so many slack-jawed

it's old women who appear all over in daylight
who climb subway steps pulling a loaded shopping cart

who burrow down the aisles of crowded moving buses
who lean on you when you do not offer them your seat

who talk loudly in rarely heard mountain dialects
who carry big animals in cat-carrying bags

whose hair has the vivid color used by teenage girls
whose diamond-clad fingers signal lady companions

whose watchful eyes let me know they see me watching them

IN YEARS TO COME

She tells me she is answering my call
from a toy store where she is looking for
something for a seven-year-old boy whose parents
live in the woods and do not allow him plastic.

I admire people who live outside convenience
but not those who force their notions on their children.

She thinks that in years to come this seven-year-old
may be the one to construct
the first all-plastic home among the conifers.

LISTENING

We are listening to the elevators
on the fifteenth floor which make different sounds
ascending and descending and when one stops
on another floor we can hear its doors
slide open and also hear behind apartment doors
voices and other sounds that we can guess at
but when one of the four elevators stops
on the fifteenth floor and its doors slide open
she runs for her life from alien invaders
but then peeks out our apartment doorway to see
what they look like while I say hello and they eye
me warily standing there in the corridor

NO SIGN OF WILLIE

Where cars park on the south side
of Madison Square Garden
abundant marijuana
smoke oozes from a bus size
recreational vehicle
with calligraphic letters
spelling out Willie Nelson
the unique country singer
with a legendary life
on the road and this of course
is a publicity stunt
and Willie himself is not
within city blocks of here

PHOTO EDIT

Here's the photo for the paperback cover,
it reveals the man in Muhammad Ali
although we must erase that mark on his cheek.

Airbrush a flaw in the world champion's skin?

Had he got it in the ring, it would remain –
a heavyweight boxer, yet the only scar
he has on his face, he got from a woman,
a broken plate in a romantic dispute.

REGULAR SHAMPOO

Murumuru butter,
amia oil extract,
exotic vegetables

and tropical berries
complicated my search
for regular shampoo.

A man ahead. A large
butterfly flexed its wings
on his left shoulder blade.

I wondered if this was
like walking a lobster
on a length of ribbon.

I asked, Is that your pet?

He glared. Is what my pet?

The butterfly perched on
the back of your collar.

His hand brushed it off and
it zigzagged in flight down
Lexington Avenue.

He plainly thought that I
had something to do with
this butterfly attack,

attaching no blame to
the huckleberry rinse
he may have been wearing.

Americas

CAPE COD

I've been to the Cape many times
and to me the place seems different
every time. Places change. This might
hold elsewhere but houses here are
a couple of centuries old.
Walls are painted (here always white)
and bushes grow. Things seem different.
Emotional maturation
I suppose could be held to blame
and think the place remains the same.

WINGED SPIRIT

The thing unnerved old New Englanders:
an owl in flight turns its head to gaze
in your face and exchanges a glance
like someone you once knew long ago
and then the owl flies away from you
with absolutely silent wing beats

JUNE MORNINGS

A camera operator told me
that on a sunny June morning in New England
she shot the spring part of a TV commercial,
a new couple in a new car
in maple woods in a valley.

She was told the next shoot, the part in fall,
was scheduled for early the next morning.

Another sunny June morning in New England
but instead of yesterday's green leafs of maple
she saw October brown, lemon yellow,
arterial crimson and dozens of colors
in a leaf peeper's autumnal panorama.

Workers in cherry pickers still applied
finishing touches from aerosol cans.

They brought in a crew from Los Angeles,
a production person said disapprovingly.

COUNTRY TRAFFIC

Not paying attention
 in a traffic delay,
I rear end a pickup,
hardly more than a tap.

Confederate decal,
long gun in the gun rack,
long faces unshaven,
blue eyes, might be brothers.

The driver slow mumbles,
I was wondering if
you done it on purpose.
I tell him I didn't.

His brother assures me,
On the farm we get hit
by mad hogs that weigh more
than any Toyota.

INSIDE LOOKING OUT, OUTSIDE LOOKING IN

Snowy egrets on delicate legs
walk in the marsh, picking here and there
with narrow bills like ladies shopping,
watched by us inside a Chevrolet,
windows up, not because of urban
instincts but because of mosquitoes
knocking their heads against the glass, their
eyes hungrily looking in at us
like things from Night of the Living Dead
knowing what we are (skin-covered blood),
and we believe they may be hatching
a new mosquitoey strategy
to get inside and eat us alive

THE FEAST OF ST. FILAMENA

Only minutes after darkness fell on Pennsylvania
we thought that we might spend the night at some motel
in this small town, which seemed unpretentious and unthreatening.

I stopped the car to make way for a procession
of hundreds of people holding flaming candles
and carrying placards of babies in the flickering light.

"They're Catholics," I said and waited for the penny to drop
but she was enchanted by the sight of so many people
singing and walking peaceably through the small town.

"What's it for?" she asked. I told her about St. Filamena,
the teenage nun in Italy who saved babies from the plague
and who has been honored for centuries all over the world.

My task now was to get her out of town before
she realized who these singing people were and
jumped from the car to scream at them about the rights of women.

The procession of candlelit singers through town
wended its way to the steps of a floodlit church
and I waited fifty miles before I told her the truth about St. Filamena.

SHOP TALK

When I heard that many there would be
professional gardeners
I expected talk to be about
flora with Latin names.

If there was any dominant theme
it was their painful knees
and what it was best to kneel upon:
knee pads or folded sacks.

HATE GROUPS

In a 2016 map published
by the Southern Poverty Law Center
with symbols representing the locations
of active hate groups in the United States
southern states are thickly coated in symbols,
Alaska and Hawaii have none,
the northwestern states have very few
(which I think of as crawling in yokels
protecting hideouts with automatic rifles),
while wilderness-free little New Jersey
festers in symbols for the Ku Klux Klan,
Racist Skinheads, White Nationalists, Neo-Nazis,
Neo-Confederates and Christian Identity.
As they say on television news: who knew?

REPELLENT

A Seven-Eleven store
kept open around the clock
heard complaints from customers
of youths lingering outside.

Bright lights did not repel them.

One man claimed he knew what would.

Play Mozart very softly
nonstop on outside speakers
and no self-respecting dude
will be caught dead for a mile.

ELLINGTON IN IOWA

Even now, many years later,
when he returns to his hometown
deep in the corn of Iowa
some people always remember
one time he was the high school kid
who brought Duke Ellington to town.

The bus from Chicago arrived
outside the graduation dance
and he recalls the band members
examining their surroundings,
polite and elegantly dressed,
among farm kids in Sunday best.

Then the band played and the kids danced
and the night happened that people
remember all these years later.
Mr. Ellington stayed formal
but as he left he shook their hands
and said this is my kind of town.

MOUNTAIN FACE

The rock face stared back aggressive as if
it did not much care for the look of me.

Apart from conifer tufts and wrinkles
made by rock slides, the face was red and raw.

I thought I saw something move halfway up,
an animal that scampered on bare rock,

two of them. They might be cougars, bears, wolves.
Bighorn sheep were a possibility.

I focused my binoculars and groaned:
one wore a green shirt, and the other blue.

LITTLE FISHES

In early hatcheries
the fry lived in a pool,
over which a dead cow's
head was hung. The maggots
that devoured the cow's head
dropped off in the water
and became salmon food.

This taught the baby fish
to wait for food to drop
from the sky. They lost their
instinct to fear shadows
of predators above.

Mothers, remember this
when you are preparing
to feed your little ones.

HELP FOR VULTURES

You know the way that vultures soar
over wilderness and mountains
without expending a wing beat
for hour after hour at a time.

Think how a transmitter attached
to scaly leg or back feathers
could enable cell phone service
in areas where vultures hang.

This might help their reputation
and change our attitude to them.

SANDWICH

I am in an East Coast hurry
for no particular reason.

Standing in line for a sandwich
at Ralphs, I am irritated
by a man I can only hear
ordering in a monotone
three sandwiches, each with something
added or taken away, one
with cress but without anchovy.

I look at the cause of delay.

Italians, Greeks and French are known
to care about ingredients
and this one is large and muscled
and coated in construction dust.

Time to think of the benefits
of Mediterranean food
with cress but without anchovy.

A PACK FORMS

Strange to see the five-year-olds
on their first baseball lesson
standing around and looking
every direction except
at the batter on home plate

but in an hour they all know
they are on opposing teams
and look in one direction
determined that while they play
the batter will go nowhere

BOB HOPE LIVES HERE

Celebrity home tour buses
in Beverly Hills often stopped
outside the dwelling of Bob Hope.

Often he obliged by taking,
in a dressing gown and slippers,
something out to a garbage can.

Bob knew only a great actor
could hold an audience spellbound
while disposing of kitchen waste.

FREEWAY

Six lanes at a gentle seventy,
hard to believe all these cars are bound
for driveways in front of modest homes,

they ease right and exit one by one,
others enter, keeping numbers up.

I think: No more exits. Stay in lane.
Mexico, wake up! We're headed south.

TARGET ONSHORE

He drove from Coronado
and ran alone for miles on
the empty ribbon of sand
below Imperial Beach.

A few gulls and wading birds …
pelicans flew in a line.

A thing bobbed on the surface,
heads, arms, then five, seven, nine
or more big men in wetsuits
crowded around him dripping.

He saw them laughing despite
their goggles and mouthpieces.

Without warning, in seconds,
they vanished into water
while he remained like something
left by the tide on the sand.

He guessed they must have been SEALs,
Navy special combat troops.

If only he had kicked one
instead of just standing there
like a petrified insect
among the laughing frogmen.

They struck black and glittering
from a blue impassive sea.

A WALK NEAR GUATEMALA

I did not care when the Indian guide
I hired hired another Indian guide
out of what I was to pay him, saying
the new man was local, a thing I had
understood the original to be.

I think he is from the mountains where we
are going, he explained and politely
had me show the new guide my revolver.
The sight of the gun made him smile. They spoke
together in what may have been Nahuatl.

We got off the bus on the highway and
walked on a path along a mountain slope.
Children greeted us at small settlements
and from adults we purchased food and drink
In the doorways of tiny stone houses.

At one place the children did not greet us.
They ran around and continued their games
as if we were invisible to them.
The adults went inside and closed their doors
without having made eye contact with us.

My guides turned around and retreated back
the way we came, closely followed by me.
We must be off this mountain before dark,
one said. Both seemed genuinely frightened.
We waited on the highway for a bus.

THE LOST FOOTSTEPS OF COL. FAWCETT

You do not walk today in the lost footsteps
of disappeared Fawcett, who knew where to find
a city of legend hid in the jungle
and who may have been hit by a blowgun dart
or have been trailed into the rainforest and
waylaid by needy thugs from a shantytown

You do not walk today in his lost footsteps
beneath long vines hanging from the canopy,
you drive a truck on dirt roads through remaining
ash and carbonized stems, it's slash and burn here
and no more worry about blowgun darts but
keep a watch for needy thugs from shantytowns

RIO

The white men on the raft in the Green River
shook their heads and fists at mounted Indians
who beckoned them to paddle toward the bank.

Then they heard the rapids before they saw them.

On a Rio street when a man shook his head
I nodded and turned back the way I had come.

BRAZILIAN PROVERB

A Brazilian translates a proverb:
In a river filled with piranhas
an alligator swims on its back.

Although there are no alligators
in Brazil, he no doubt used this word
for reptiles with soft underbellies

and knew that saltwater crocodiles
in Amazon estuaries fear
only others and tyrannosaurs.

Ireland

LIONS WITH LAMBS

Rabbits ignore
people swinging
long-handled clubs
in lush grass at
Parknasilla.

When playing golf
what causes folk
in rabbits' eyes
to abandon
humanity?

A WHITE HORSE AT KENMARE RIVER

You are beautiful,
a white horse motionless on the green grass
with some green trees waving in the background.

You stand still, continue looking at us.

Are you curious?
I know you horses like to look over
a half door at anything happening.

Perhaps you want to come back home with us.

People who rode horses in Central Park
once stabled them on the Upper West Side
and horses placidly climbed staircases
to lodging places.

Tell me, would you have a problem with that?

Although I cannot recall any saint
having a vision of a horse, are you
alerting us that it is time for our
spirits to awake?

Eat some grass. Why are you looking at us?

NO LONELY GRAVE

My uncle waited at the open grave
in the churchyard with other Catholics,
neighbors of the dead Protestant farmer,
while the prayers were said and hymns were sung
in the Church of Ireland at Clonoulty.

Nine years old, I wandered away to look
at two gravediggers dig another grave,
who ignored the city boy onlooker
apart from throwing an occasional
spadeful of earth over my polished shoes.

I watched for the thing they would uncover:
soon they cleared the earth from the varnished wood
still gleaming as if only yesterday,
a digger threw me a gravedigger's look
and raised his spade and smote the coffin lid.

It vanished in dust, exposing a bleached
skeleton neatly arrayed on its back,
and they spaded earth to cover the bones
and scattered handfuls of hay on this floor,
a welcome mat for the new occupant.

KORINGA, THE JUNGLE GIRL

A girl with almost no clothes alone
on a table, a laundry basket,
beneath a light in a circus ring.

What would this American circus
release here in Catholic Ireland?

A python ten feet long, a body
thick as my own, crawled from the basket.

She and the snake moved this way and that
to make each other comfortable
on the tabletop as Egyptian
music swirled and thudded in the dark.

Although very young I knew I would
when she half-opened her eyes and said,
Bring me the head of John the Baptist.

CELLO

My cousin had a German boyfriend who played the cello
in the symphony orchestra and talked about the sound
in a large high-ceilinged ground floor room of my cousin's home,
where he liked to practice and I sometimes got to listen
to him struggle with the instrument and recording wire.

Every now and then he stopped playing and cursed and shouted
in German, waved his bow around and even stamped a foot.

When I now hear one of J.S. Bach's solo cello suites
on the radio I feel that if the player would stop
once in a while to berate his playing it might only
add to listener satisfaction at his performance.

NEAR FETHARD

At evening, across a field,
we heard a church bell pealing,
weak and small and soon fading.

That's from the graveyard, he said.

I knew his cousins were brought
here at times for burial.

I had not seen a belfry
in the neglected graveyard,
now it was too dark to see.

Alone the next day I climbed
over tombs and through high weeds,
found a rectangle of stones,
walls less than eight feet high that
might have been a tiny church.

It made sense the bell sounded
weak and small and soon faded.

A FARMHOUSE YEARS AGO

The smell of geraniums
three shelves high in the glasshouse
warmed by an ovenlike sun
permeated the rooms of
the farmhouse, and now that smell
recreates a place, a time,
people gone without a trace
but for the powerful breath
of summer geraniums

CLAY WALLS

My friend Femie van den Bosch
wrote that during a dry spell in Holland
dikes had been sprayed with water
to prevent clay from crumbling.

This reminded me of the thatched cottage
I visited as a child near Ballagh
and visited again decades later
in a mood of nostalgia.

I knew people, goats and ducks
would be gone – but what I had not foreseen
was there would be no trace that
earthen walls had once stood there.

Witheroe, father of ancient Lizzie,
erected the clay-walled straw-roofed cottage,
a stone mason come to build
the railway station at Goold's Cross, long closed.

They say he may have hailed from Aberdeen,
where the houses are built of
cut granite blocks that will make
long-lasting skeletal remains one day.

NEGLECT BORDERING ON RUIN

The stag on the moor in that painting
has moved forward since I have been here.

The carpet is damp, wallpaper too.

The bronze candelabrum might impress
but there is no electric power.

The mantelpiece is gone, exposing
raw brick beneath the vanished marble.

How long have ashes lain in the grate?

But I feel no dread of the unknown.

If a ghost ever haunted this room
that ghost has long abandoned the place.

CELTS

They spoke languages close to modern Welsh
south to Verona and almost to Rome
in Julius Caesar's day. They were Celts.

They might have come as a horde from the Steppes,
naked, skins blue, on half-broken horses,
hair in the wind, with yells, aiming lances.

But no carbon, bone or weapon fragments
mark their arrival, so one person said
or wrote: There were no Celts. They never came.

Around the time they were supposed to have
invaded Europe, the use of iron
was spreading north and west, replacing bronze.

What if Celtic languages came along
with the use of iron and spread with it
in the way computers favor English?

Celts never came. Now Celtic languages,
far from city life and technology,
die creepingly. Soon there will be no Celts.

TWO NURSES

Two nurses in front of a shelled building
in Dublin after the Easter Rising
in 1916. They pose side by side
before rubble beyond restoration
with a bicycle between them, armbands
with a cross. The one in nurse's outfit
looks at the camera, the other smiles
politely to the photographer's left
in a dark-colored Victorian dress.
The nurses know this is no-woman's land.

POPE GEORGE

You don't have to be a priest to be made pope
and what if they elect me pope in springtime?

Why would they choose me as pope? Because I could
renew the church in one move: Make women priests.

Think about all the old things that need dusting.
Women would have no problem clearing the mess.

LOYAL DAUGHTER

The Donegal poet
Madge Herron wrote that her
father had become
bereft of reason.

The clothesline in his head
where all his flags hung out
to dry had now collapsed.

She wouldn't do a thing
that might interfere with
how he was constructed.

She didn't want to see
her father full of holes
with scores of dead sheep
pouring out of him.

A NICE SOFT DAY

Showers come and go, rain doesn't last
or so we hope, it's a nice soft day,
so we say, it's keeping the grass green,
doesn't all the constant watering
keep Dublin clean, while Los Angeles
bakes in the sun and people have to
oil themselves to avoid skin cancer,
drink ice water to hydrate their cells
and darken their vision so that rays
do not burn the middle of their eyes,
we sympathize and we empathize
while we enjoy the crystalline glint
of the rainwater on chilled granite

A MONAGHAN MAN

I wondered who could have let him wander
in a city, he looked straight off the farm
and spoke with a strong Monaghan accent
that made him hard at times to understand.

He said he had been home on two visits
in nearly three decades and spoke English
only once or twice a year where he lived,
a priest in the Peruvian Andes.

He went to bring Christ to the Quechua
and after twentysomething years emerged
Monaghan in perfect preservation.

Other Places

MIDSUMMER DAY

On midsummer day in an English market town
the building stones and walls beneath a cloudless sky
have reticence and protective coloration.

Not so the tiny gardens around cottages
with their freehand throws of seeds that bloomed as comets,
golden stands of shrinking virgins, new rich crimson
loudmouths and forceful green shoots with broad hairy leaves
that some believe may flower in time for Christmas.

ENGLISH HOTEL

On a wall near the desk, bells in rows,
each hung on a single coil steel spring
marked by room in old fashioned numbers,
were activated by wire pulleys.

Good to see no one had altered what
may have been an ostentatious show
of the latest in technology
for indolent Victorian guests.

A bell rang from number twenty-five.
The clerk keyed his telephone and spoke.
In the old days a servant would have
climbed the stairs and knocked on the room door.

In my room I tugged on a handmade
beaded needlepoint bell pull. The phone
rang. The clerk spoke, polite but weary:
You may telephone directly, sir.

UNIDENTIFIED STRUCTURES

South of London on the North Downs
in a dip in the grassy hills
two half-cylinders two men high
of rusting corrugated zinc
and leveled ground that leads nowhere –
one could wonder why they are here
like a circle of standing stones.

Near one of the two Nissen huts
there could have been a metal plaque
bearing the words that Churchill spoke:
Never in the field of human conflict
was so much owed by so many to so few.

There could have been a replica
of a Spitfire on the runway.

There could have been a monument
but there are only butterflies
and larks that soar high in the breeze.

ON FIRST HEARING MARGARET BARRY

They slept eight hours, worked eight hours, drank four hours,
took buses in between, from rooming house

to building site to noisy Irish pub
in Camden Town, and did so every day.

They saw themselves as country lads who did
the heavy work the English could not do.

Noise in the pub died when a small woman
with a bottle of stout, an empty glass

and a banjo made her way to a chair
on a foot-high platform next to a wall.

Some exchanged words with her as she passed by,
most only smiled in anticipation.

She was a Traveler woman and might
have sung at many a rowdy camp fire.

Margaret quieted discordant men
with loud dissonant chords on the banjo.

They might once have heard a voice like hers from
a ring fort or a tumbledown graveyard.

With tattered old songs from another time
her sly rawness brought them back to the fields.

GREEN AND ORANGE

Most Englishmen considered all of us
Paddies, regardless of whether we were
from the republic or fellow British
citizens from Ulster. We were Paddies,
each and every one of us. Ulstermen
could enjoy the bitter humor of this.

But they did not enjoy republicans
and let us know it without much humor
in the workplace. One night I was surprised
to encounter four of the most hostile
drinking pints in a nationalist pub.
We all nodded at the bitter humor.

They correctly guessed I would say nothing.
No looks of understanding were exchanged
in the workplace on later days. Had I
been knocked to the floor in a work dispute,
I think they would have kicked me, but only
to show each wore a loyal British boot.

ROYAL EVENT

The lawn at the rear of Buckingham Palace
for a garden party
contains hundreds of people in their best clothes
holding umbrellas and
standing politely in a steady downpour

while the queen in a fuchsia coat and puce hat
holding her umbrella
unhurriedly circulates among her guests

WHITECHAPEL GALLERY

The Whitechapel Gallery some years ago
showed things that expected things of you, no more
just looking at trees or breasts or the moon, you
participated and you had things to do
and it could be fun when not too cerebral.

Today the gallery seemed to be concerned
with community affairs and its young staff
were unconventionally groomed and clothed.

The only visitor, I walked out the door
with an expectation of the usual
dense London traffic on Whitechapel High Street.

It was empty. I waited solitary
as a visiting foreign dignitary
who has no one to welcome him, the police
I could see at opposite ends of the street
keeping onlookers behind plastic ribbons.

A uniform ran toward me. A bomb threat,
he warned me. I knew then that this probably
was real. It was too large scale to be work
of artists from the Whitechapel Gallery.

LONDON RESTING PLACES

1
Brompton Cemetery

Large angels are few,
as are lifesize statues
of despairing women.

Solitary men
take the accustomed place
of angels and women.

Do the living give
the dead the notion they
have not been forgotten?

2
Highgate Cemetery

George Eliot was here before Karl Marx
but his giant head is the biggest stone
and when you look at other stones you see
how socialists and communists who sought
twentieth century London refuge
having had their people politics crushed
nestle in earth beds around their thinker
himself a philosopher in exile

3
Moravian Burial Ground

A man eating salad from a plastic box
for lunch on a bench in the sun claimed that he
had grown up in nearby Redcliffe Gardens and
had never known the barred gate to be unlocked
at the bend in King's Road close to the World's End.

Now this once hidden place is open Wednesday,
God's acre of mowed grass with level stone plaques
in line equidistantly placed feet apart.
Beneath each of the plaques a Moravian
buried erect waits for Resurrection Day.

The Royal Borough of Chelsea has been hit
by a force seven Himalayan earthquake.
A man stands waist deep in his burial hole,
his hands on the grass, with these thoughts in his head:
Is this it? Was that the sound of the last trump?
Is it time to go?

IN THE DARK

One saw a mask, the she-wolf's of old Rome,
the ears, the brow, the cold unpitying eyes

One heard the spider's fatal purring,
trumpeting of gray mammoths locked in ice

The moon outside the window
I am near a wall

I know there is a carpet
sheets upon the bed

I do not reach my fingers
for fear they might touch

things that go bump in the night
in a wookey hole

WOMEN ON BICYCLES

Long-boned women ride tall old-fashioned bicycles
and take blind corners at high speed in Amsterdam.
I watched two collide and lie on the street. They laughed
and helped each other pick up scattered packages.
They may have exchanged some shopping information.

CITY OF SPECTRES

In 1854
Apollonie and Charles

were strolling arm in arm
beneath a cloudless moon

night streamed like a river
over sleeping Paris

from under a railing
two black cats appeared and

slowly walked beside them

spirit familiars

BURGUNDY AFTERNOON

You speak English? he asked disdainfully,
with almost correct pronunciation.
Private. You cannot eat your *picnic* here.
He eyed the label on the wine bottle
among the terrines, fromage and baguettes.
Clos de Vougeot, he murmured, his fight gone.
You wish to drink wine where its grapes were grown?
Well, you have come to the wrong place.
Your wine comes from over there, rows away.
These vines are mine. But you have a good wine –
he cares for his vines, unlike some others.
There are more than fifty of us here, if
you count those who own less than a full row.
I hate looking at vines. I see the work
they require or the neglect they suffer,
pitiful arms hanging on wires and stakes.
It's complicated when you know
which vine rows do not speak to which
or which are married or have been allied
for generations. All of Burgundy
is in these vines and the wall around them.
Monks built the wall to keep the sinners out.
Caesar was here two thousand years ago –
I've seen men in togas inspect these vines
in sunlight and dissolve into the leaves.
But I must go. Enjoy your meal.

A PLACE TO REST

He's not from this village and he hanged himself
over a young woman's grave, dead only days.

The priest refuses him a church burial,
the mayor says his people should come for him.

He is stretched on a table in a back room.

Today being the third day, we need to take
him outdoors. The sheet will keep away the flies.

This evening I'll go with friends to bury him
near a row of vines outside the graveyard wall.

The Hennessys own the land and they won't mind.

Sometimes I believe there must be as many
lying outside as inside in holy ground.

OLD SOLDIER

Pakistani soldier
in the British army,
he survived World War II.

Back home in Pakistan,
he told the children that
he would shoot an angel
if any came for him.

When he turned ninety-one
an angel arrived and
he could not find his gun.

Wannabe Haiku

Helicopters drop
      hay to deer on the mountain
            and the snow is fat

    *

Park Avenue in
      autumn a doorman reaches
            for the fallen leaf

    *

Ireland the rain is
      not falling out of the sky
            but dropping gently

    *

The cat watches with
      half its face and one green eye
            what you are doing

    *

Tablecloth removed
      a cat is examining
            the wood tabletop

    *

The cat paws the crumbs
      across the tabletop and
            waits for them to run

    *

A young woman wears
        a rolled up mat on her back
                prayer or yoga

        *

Alone does she know
        beneath cascading cherry
                that she is dancing?

        *

Allergic to plants,
        with a telephoto lens
                she keeps her distance

        *

Lemon, I see none,
        so she points out the window
                at a lemon tree

        *

Please clear the way for
        the small dog with a long stick
                crosswise in its mouth

        *

Concoct such a word
        as sphygmomanometer
                no poet today

        *

Long remembered by
        junk mail that keeps arriving
                after we are gone

        *

Life size, cast in bronze,
        an equestrian statue
                melted into guns

      *

Sacrificial sock
        in the hot rotating drum
                of a clothes dryer

      *

The water surface
        as leaves crawl across its face
                may be quivering

      *

The water insects
        conduct their three-hour-flightlife
                aerial orgies

      *

They may look trapped but
        fruitflies can run through the knot
                in a plastic bag

      *

Tail to a comet
        of broken mosquito legs
                a smear of dried blood

      *

Left in a famine
        dogs howling in empty homes
                the last island sounds

      *

They say in Haiti,
        a fish trusts the water and
                is cooked in water

        *

Bougainvillea
        a passion of red flowers
                spilling over walls

        *

Rolling downhill fast,
        clutching the bike handlebars,
                a small boy, eyes wide

        *

Try not to say a
        four-letter word the children
                might throw in your face

        *

He is bewildered,
        his wife embroidered inside
                all his suit pockets

        *

The gravel is dragged
        loudly by waves as the sea
                hoarsely clears its throat

        *

I think that he said
        her hears are awed of earring
                or something like that

        *

Only imagine
        the tranquil vacuity
                of a wakeful mind

Half the Fat, No Sugar

I BELIEVE YOU, A THOUSAND WOULDN'T

1
I have nothing against people who bring
their screaming infants inside a sports bar –
they can't be heard when a good game is on

2
I try to keep this sound advice in mind:
if you cannot be honest with yourself
at least be honest with other people

3
After two whole weeks
below freezing in New York

you lower the car window
in Los Angeles

and scents rush in like
perfume sprayed in Bloomingdales

SAY NOTHING AND I'LL BE YOUR FRIEND FOREVER

1
The ding and dong and ding and dong:
the elfin hammer blows of rhyme
that lead us merrily along
to hear the bells we know that chime.

But find totem rhymed with scrotum,
ask what elves are now in elfdom.

2
I remember that time when you
repeatedly knocked on the wall
and loudly wailed your daughter's name
in a cold early morning hour
so the newly arrived couple
in the apartment next to yours
wondered if the place was haunted

3
The cat has jumped from the boxes
to the tabletop and now stands
with the tablecloth rising up
around her like Marilyn's dress
when she was caught in that updraft

4
Corroded sheets of corrugated steel
for a roof, hardly enough to keep out
the wind and rain

with massive supporting I-beam pillars,
enough to withstand itchy haunches of
wintering cows

NO DOGS, NO DUMPING, NO LOUD MUSIC

1
Walk the plank, scallywag!
a kid in pirate hat
yells at me as he waves
a plastic Roman sword.

You would be impressed by
how we pass along our
cultural traditions.

2
You can't watch grass grow
in New York City
but you can always
watch concrete harden

3
Like a woman.

Like two womans.

4
There is a laundry god
who you must pacify
and whose demand you meet:
a sock as sacrifice

5
Perched on a branch
above water,
a night heron
stares fixedly
with blood-red eyes

ANTS ATTACK VATICAN

1
A helicopter is first to arrive, circling
downriver from the bridge. Two or three squad cars park
on a span, multicolor roof lights revolving.
Two boats come, each one with a blue light of mourning.

2
At a glance I'd say there are too many people
on that beach, but you say they are worshippers
gathered at the confluence of the Ganges
and other rivers, I say too many people

3
Last week the soup cans were two aisles over,
spaghetti was near the tomato sauce,
what happened to the unmodified milk,
I know they do this to mess with my mind

4
Why do I ignore
Irish traffic signs
that tell me GO SLOW
but obey the ones
that say REDUCE SPEED?

5
Hilarious ... Charming ... Heartfelt ...
Adjectives that may explain why
I don't remember this movie.

FILLING IN OPEN PIT MINES WITH PLASTIC CUPS

1
Suddenly asked if I expect
to live beyond my death somehow
I say no as most people do

but I've heard that the pope has said
atheists can go to heaven

2
The chicken noodle soup
had turned to a green mush
in the can

which was gross till I saw
I had opened a can
of split pea

3
This time of year, she said,
you can tell the people
with small children. We talk
of witches, masks, cobwebs,
carving eyes in pumpkins.
Others need a moment.

4
When I returned in hope to the supermarket
a woman held up a manila envelope
she knew I had forgotten in my shopping cart
because she and I had been through this already
several times.

You can leave an envelope containing poems
and no one will ever take it, I told someone,
who said that leaving poems in supermarkets
could not be looked on as an effective way to
distribute them.

PRESS 1 FOR ENGLISH

1
Ledhrblaka
leatherflapper
and fledermaus
one side of bat
and another
is pipistrelle

2
I heard her say in a low growl,
Me and you can live in this place
without me sitting on papers
or walking over your keyboard
or climbing up on your shoulder,
all you got to do, it's simple,
it's no big demand, is feed me.

3
He wonders why people don't believe him
when he tells them he drinks less nowadays
and thus has a reduced capacity
and appears drunk more often than before

IS YOU OR IS YOU AIN'T

1
Her year-old grandson crawling on the floor,
a thread dangling from his mouth, which she pulled
and out popped an angel, an ornament
he could not swallow because of its wings

2
Daylight lengthens and ducks
moving north attempt mock
random mating charges

but no Manhattan gulls
willingly tolerate
spring fever from swamp ducks

3
As Blaise Pascal once wrote:
Their imagination
cannot make madmen wise
but it makes them happy.

4
Jed Perl caught flight and said Alexander
Calder's aerial mobiles
have elements and groups of elements
unfolding and unfurling
in different directions at different rates

BECOME A NEW YOU

1
You post a picture
on Facebook of how a violent wind
knocked down the gazebo in your backyard
and someone assumes
it is the aftermath of a party

2
When they caught him they opened
his suitcase and discovered
a piece of America

3
It seems I have been added to
the early morning list of things to do
the cat keeps mentally.

Heretofore inactivity
has protected me.

Lack of response would seem
the only way that I can dream
of losing my listed place
and not being licked on the face
with bats around
before roosters sound.

THINK YOU'RE IN HEAVEN BUT YOU'RE LIVING IN HELL

1
A little goldfish can give companionship.

For a frequent traveler it's easier
to find someone to look after a goldfish.

2
Over coffee and apple pastry
a woman talks in slow High German
to another woman who answers
in highly grammatical English.

It can be hard to find Germans who
don't want to try their English on you.

3
Have you really lost it when you can't
twist the cap off a miniature
whisky bottle on an airplane flight
and a stewardess does it for you?

4
The cramped space into which John Glenn was squeezed
as he orbited in *Friendship 7*
now at the Smithsonian museum
is lovingly commemorated by
the commercial airline I fly today

YOU HAVE BEEN PRESELECTED

1
A person claimed that in
society today
fifteen percent teeter
on each extremist wing
while seventy percent
wobble in the middle

2
In a town in New Mexico
the poet Richard Shelton saw
that professional prostitutes
no longer dressed much better than
schoolteachers, their income lowered
by competition from all the
enthusiastic amateurs

3
We can rely on Frank to bring
a two-liter plastic bottle of vodka
from which he will pour a liberal measure
into offered glasses and carefully add
from a very much smaller plastic bottle
raw organic liquefied fruits
while praising their health benefits
in spite of their sometimes high sugar levels

4
I admit I am appalled at Arthur's
notion to erect apartment buildings
on pilings above extensive graveyards
in Queens on what was once the eastern edge
of New York City out on Long Island

FROM THE COMFORT OF HOME

1
Anyone whose poems are rejected
by magazines knows the phrase editors
are apt to use: Your poems do not fit …

They are polite but reveal a mindset
in expectation that poems should fit.

2
A London friend with a broken leg
claims that he was hit by the Rolls-Royce
of a member of the House of Lords.

Another friend says that he was hit
by a schoolgirl on a bicycle.

3
You say it's not the waiting, sir,
it's the music while you're waiting.
I can't hear music at this end.
What kind of music is it, sir?

An unsuccessful Broadway show.

That bad? It could explain the mood
of some folk when I talk to them.

4
Doing ninety.

Kilometers.

Minutes later:

No, they are not.

Not what?

Kilometers.

NO BAD LANGUAGE, EROTICA, VIOLENCE, NOTHING DISTURBING

1
The tails of planes stick out of hangars
like horses' heads looking out of stalls.

Wrong way in, they can find no way out.

2
It doesn't matter what you plant, everything grows,
and it doesn't matter when you plant it. That was
a California gardener's opinion
as she stood in her lemon trees and rosemary.

3
That's a television reporter
on view in wind and rain while struggling
to find the words to express himself

4
I will not buy oil for the hinges
of the folding composition wood
linen closet doors that groaningly
creak like wrought iron in an oak door
hung in a resounding cut stone arch

AMISH COUNTRY CAGE-FREE LARGE BROWN EGGS

1
The kid wanted a pirate Christmas tree,
which made his mother smile, until she saw
the skull and crossbones he made for the top

2
The only electronic process
that so far baffles Russian hackers
is how they can borrow an ebook
from the New York Public Library

3
Two photos because
she could never get
all four
of her young children
to look
at the camera
at a single time

4
You are approaching eighty:
abandon beekeeping and
navigation by the stars
as things you may need to know

5
Floating down the river,
a barge has letters
painted on its side.

I put on spectacles
and read BNLP,
not what I first thought.

**Placement of poems in complete poems
(with page numbers from *Surprised by Gulls* for reference)**

Americas
Cape Cod [after IN NORTH EGREMONT p 132]
Winged Spirit
June Mornings
Country Traffic [after ALABAMA 1964 p 137]
Inside Looking Out, Outside Looking In [after EASTERN SHORE p 138]
The Feast of St. Filamena [after GOING BACK p 153]
Shop Talk [after LOOKING FOR WALTER, p 154]
Hate Groups
Repellent
Ellington in Iowa
Mountain Face [after THEY HUNT TO EAT p 159]
Little Fishes
Hope for Vultures
Sandwich [after HOLY FAMILY p 165]
A Pack Forms
Bob Hope Lives Here
Freeway
Target Onshore [after THE BRIDE p 166]
A Walk Near Guatemala [after LONE SWIMMER p 172]
The Lost Footsteps of Col. Fawcett
Rio
Brazilian Proverb

Ireland
Lions with Lambs [after GOING SOUTH p 230]
A White Horse at Kenmare River
No Lonely Grave [after PENS MIGHTIER THAN SWORDS p 237]
Koringa, the Jungle Girl [after DUBLIN HALLOWEEN LONG GONE p 238]
Cello [after CHANT p 240]
Near Fethard [after GIRAFFES p 241]
A Farmhouse Years Ago [after THE TIME IN AUSTRALIA p 245]
Clay Walls
Neglect Bordering on Ruin
Celts
Two Nurses
Pope George
Loyal Daughter
A Nice Soft Day
A Monaghan Man

Other Places
Midsummer Day [after WINNER p 252]
English Hotel
Unidentified Structures
On First Hearing Margaret Barry
Green and Orange
Royal Event [after CEREMONIAL DUTY p 254]
Whitechapel Gallery
London Resting Places
In the Dark
Women on Bicycles [after ORBIT p 256]
City of Spectres [after BEASTS p 258]
Burgundy Afternoon [after AROMA p 259]
A Place to Rest
Old Soldier [after DESERT HOMECOMING p 269]